C000171316

Henderson's
Book of
Salads

Henderson's Book of Salads

Illustrations by
Maggie Williams

Northern Books
from Famedram

ISBN 978-0-905489-94-0
© Copyright 2003, 2005, 2014 Famedram Publishers Ltd

Not to be reproduced in any form without written authorisation from the publishers.
Published by Famedram Publishers Ltd, PO Box 3, AB41 9EA
www.northernbooks.co.uk
Print: Imprint Digital Ltd

Contents

It is important that you remember to wash any salad ingredients and vegetables thoroughly before use and, when possible, try to use local organic produce

Foreword

ALONG WITH its companion publication Henderson's
Wholefood Cookbook, Henderson's Book of Salads has
become an established favourite on kitchen bookshelves.

Both titles are regularly refreshed and reprinted so they
can reveal to new generations of cooks the secrets that
have built the reputation of this much-loved Edinburgh
institution over more than half a century.

Henderson's
Book of Salads

Introduction

THE YEAR 2013 was a memorable one for Henderson's. It marked the fiftieth anniversary of the founding of the famous Hanover Street institution and provided an excellent excuse for a party – indeed a whole series of celebrations took place.

It had been the same ten years earlier, in October 2003, to celebrate the fact that, forty years back Janet and Mac Henderson had first opened up their shop in Edinburgh.

A profusion of delicious wholefood produce was being grown on their East Lothian farm and they needed somewhere to sell it. Day by day more and more carloads of organic fruit and vegetables were despatched to the shop in Hanover Street. Soon Janet Henderson cast her eyes on the basement premises beneath the shop.

It seemed like the perfect place for a wholefood restaurant selling meals made from the sort of fresh wholesome food that was on sale in the shop above. Henderson's Salad Table restaurant was born.

It was this vision that was being celebrated by the great and good of Edinburgh half a century on.

For the 40th birthday Edinburgh's Lord Provost was there with his memories. He could, he said, remember visiting Henderson's in the early seventies, but he had a sneaking suspicion that his motives might not have been of the purest.

Could it have been the chance of a late night 'swallow' that had attracted him rather that the prospect of virtuous, wholefood sustenance? Always innovative, Henderson's had been one of the first eating places in Edinburgh to boast a late night licence.

Many of those assembled for these celebrations, now leading lights in their own fields, once served their time in the celebrated kitchens. Henderson's has always had a polyglot outlook and at any time the roll call of helpers on board can read like a UN delegation.

In one fairly typical week this (in no particular order) was the list of nationalities represented in the kitchens and out on the floor: Italian, Spanish, Venezuelan, Brazilian, Polish, French, Australian, Egyptian, American, Irish, Canadian, Swedish, Chinese, New Zealander, Indian, Icelandic, Scottish and even some English!

Over the years Henderson's has stayed faithful to the guiding principles of its founders. It still continues very much as a family business. Local suppliers are always favoured against their larger names and the décor has been kept broadly the same, resisting the major 'themed' makeovers that have become a depressing feature of so many eating places.

At the fortieth celebration first to arrive and almost the last to leave was co-founder 'Mac' Henderson himself. Though he reached the grand old age of 101, Mac sadly did not live to join the fiftieth birthday jollities, though the founders' guiding principles still shine down strongly through the years. All that healthy eating and organic farming seems to pay dividends.

Primarily Proteins

Date, Watercress and Cheese Classic

Egg Mayonnaise

Feta, Cucumber, Olive Salad

Smoked Tofu Salad Tiede with Savoury Dressing

Date, Watercress and Cheese

INGREDIENTS
1 bunch watercress, washed, trimmed and chopped roughly
2 tomatoes, cut into wedges
100g (4oz) dates, stoned and chopped
100g (4oz) cheddar cheese, cubed

METHOD
Combine all ingredients in a generously sized bowl to
thoroughly mix flavours.

SERVES 2

14

Egg Mayonnaise

INGREDIENTS
4 eggs, hard boiled and shelled
30mls (2 tbspns) natural yoghurt
15mls (1 tbspn) mayonnaise
Approx 12 green olives
Paprika for dusting
Small pinch of salt
Freshly milled black pepper

METHOD
Quarter the eggs and arrange in serving bowl.

In a smaller bowl combine the yoghurt and the mayonnaise and adjust seasoning if required. Spoon mayonnaise mix over eggs and scatter with olives and paprika.

Serve immediately or chill.

SERVES 3-4

Feta, cucumber, olive salad

INGREDIENTS
100g (4oz) feta cheese, cut into chunks
Half a cucumber, cut into chunks
12 black olives
6 cherry tomatoes, halved
30mls (2 tbspns) French dressing
Freshly milled black pepper

METHOD
Arrange salad ingredients in a bowl and season with
pepper. Drizzle with French dressing and serve.

SERVES 2-3

Smoked Tofu Salad Tiede with Savoury Dressing

INGREDIENTS

1 packet (250g) smoked tofu, diced
50mls olive oil
15mls (1 tbspn) lemon juice
1 tspn heather honey
10mls (1 dtspn) vegetarian Ross-shire sauce
Bunch of herbs: parsley and chives.
Small pinch of salt
Freshly milled black pepper
Selection of leaves: lettuce, rocket, and salad burnet or oak leaf
3 spring onions, sliced
Quarter cucumber, sliced

METHOD

In a small saucepan infuse dressing ingredients – oil, juice, honey, seasoning, sauce and whisk them all together.

In a large bowl, combine all prepared salad ingredients. Tear herbs roughly rather than chopping for appearance and for flavour.

Lift servings onto individual plates and pour over warmed whisked dressing just prior to serving.

SERVES 2

Grains and Pulses

With grains, and particularly pulses, it is very important that they are cooked thoroughly. The beans are cooked when they crush under the pressure of your finger and thumb when squeezed. Alternatively there are very good tinned ready-cooked beans available from Henderson's shop. Cooked bean weights shown. For raw beans use half the weight.

Curried Rice Salad

Hawaiian Bean Salad

Henderson's Classic Rice Salad

Mediterranean Style Couscous.

Mixed Bean Salad

Organic Roasted Vegetable Couscous

Puy Lentil Salad

Spiced Chickpea and Olive Salad

Curried Rice Salad

INGREDIENTS
100g (4oz) wholegrain rice
3 sticks celery, sliced
1 orange, peeled and segmented
Half a pineapple, peeled and chopped
A small bunch of grapes
25g (1oz) raisins
Small pinch of salt

DRESSING:
125mls soured cream
2 tspn curry powder
30mls (2 tbspns) orange juice
1 tbspn chutney

METHOD
Cook rice in a pan of boiling lightly salted water, according to the instructions on the packet – allow about 40 minutes.

Meanwhile make the dressing by placing soured cream in a bowl along with spice and juice. Whisk gently with a fork to blend ingredients and, when smooth, stir in the chutney. Place remaining ingredients into a bowl and pour over dressing.

Once the rice has cooked, drain and add to bowl (allow rice to cool a little if time allows). Combine with the other ingredients. Ideally leave for 20 minutes to absorb flavours, however keep chilled until 10 minutes before serving.

SERVES 3

Hawaiian Bean Salad

INGREDIENTS

225g (8oz) beans – a mix of kidney beans, black eye beans,
   chickpeas, cooked and drained
1 green pepper, de-seeded and sliced
1 small red onion, peeled and sliced
One quarter of pineapple, peeled and chopped
75g (3oz) green beans
A walnut sized piece of fresh ginger, peeled and grated
1 clove garlic, peeled and crushed
30mls (2 tbspns) French dressing

METHOD

Blanch green beans in boiling
water for a couple of minutes
then drain and refresh with cold
water. Place beans in a mixing
bowl – if using canned
beans remember to drain off
any liquid. Add all remaining
ingredients and mix together.

   Ideally set aside for at least
20 minutes to allow flavours to
absorb.

SERVES 3

Henderson's Classic Rice salad

Ingredients
225g (8oz) wholegrain rice
50g (2oz) each of peppers, carrots and courgettes
30mls (2 tbspn) soy sauce
15mls (1 tbspn) olive oil
Freshly milled black pepper
Small pinch of salt

Method
Cook rice in a pan of boiling lightly salted water according to the instructions on the packet – until rice is al dente.

Meanwhile chop the vegetables to a fairly small dice. These can be eaten raw, or alternatively sautéed off quickly in a pan with the olive oil.

Once cooked drain the rice and place in a generous serving dish. Add seasoning, soy, vegetables and oil to taste. Ideally leave for 20 minutes to absorb flavours and keep chilled until 10 minutes before serving.

Serves 4

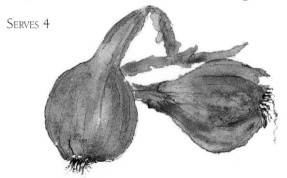

Mediterranean Style Couscous

INGREDIENTS
100g (4oz) couscous combined with equal volume of
    boiling vegetable stock
1 tspn vegetable bouillon powder (if required for stock)
20mls (2 dtsp) olive oil
1 small onion, peeled and finely chopped
1 clove garlic, peeled and crushed
1 medium courgette, cut in chunks
4 sticks celery, cut into chunks
Small pinch of freshly milled salt and pepper
25g (1oz) flaked almonds
8-10 black olives

TO GARNISH
Approx 2 tspns chopped parsley
and coriander
Lemon wedges

METHOD:
Place couscous in a bowl and pour over boiling
vegetable stock. Stir with a fork and set aside
for 10 minutes. Fluff up the grains with a fork.
Meanwhile lightly sauté vegetables in some oil.

Add all remaining ingredients, along with sautéed
vegetables, to your couscous. Combine flavours and
garnish.

Serve immediately hot or serve cold as a salad.

SERVES 2-3

Mixed Bean Salad

50g (2oz) French beans/mangetout, washed (and blanched
   if preferred)
225g (8oz) beans – a mix of kidney beans, pinto beans,
   and Cannellini beans, cooked and drained
2 medium tomatoes, cut into wedges
30mls (2 tbspns) Henderson's Tomato Dressing

Method:
In a large bowl combine all ingredients with the dressing
and leave for an hour if possible to allow beans to absorb
all the flavours. Serve with a green salad.

Serves 2

Organic Roasted Vegetable Couscous

INGREDIENTS

175g (6oz) couscous combined with equal volume of boiling water
15mls (1 tbspn) olive oil
1 clove garlic, peeled and crushed
Half a mild chilli pepper, deseeded and sliced finely
1 pepper, deseeded and cut into 1cm strips
1 red onion, peeled and coarsely chopped
100g (4oz) mushrooms, quartered
12 black olives
15mls (1 tbspn) chopped coriander and parsley
Freshly milled black pepper
Small pinch of salt
30mls (2 tbspns) French dressing
1 lemon

METHOD

Pre-heat oven to 190°C (375°F/Gas Mark 5). Toss garlic, chilli, pepper, onion and mushrooms in the scant oil and open roast on a baking tray for 10 minutes. Give the tray a gentle shake halfway through cooking time to evenly cook.

Meanwhile place couscous in a generously sized bowl and add equivalent volume of boiling water. Fluff up with a fork and set aside for the liquid to absorb. Once the couscous is ready, combine all the ingredients apart from the lemon and serve warm or cold with wedges of lemon.

SERVES 3-4

Puy Lentil Salad

225g (8oz) puy lentils
1 medium carrot, scraped and cut into strips
1 medium courgette, cut into strips
2 stalks of celery, sliced
Freshly milled black pepper
Small pinch of salt
A medium bowl of washed assorted salad leaves – Radicchio, oakleaf, Lollo Rosso

METHOD

To cook puy lentils, soak overnight in cold water. Drain and boil in a pan of boiling water until lentils are tender – soft but not mushy. In a medium bowl, combine all ingredients except the leaves, season and taste. Drizzle with a little olive oil if wished.

Line bowls with the salad leaves and spoon in lentil mixture.

SERVES 4

Spiced Chickpea and Olive Salad

Ingredients
225g (8oz) cooked chickpeas, drained
Quarter of a cucumber, diced
4 radishes, sliced
1 red onion, peeled and chopped
15mls (1 tbspn) olive oil
Dash of balsamic vinegar
1 clove garlic, crushed
15mls (1 tbspn) chopped coriander
75g (3oz) olives – black and green mix
Freshly milled black pepper
Small pinch of salt

Method
Combine all ingredients in a bowl, except the herbs, and leave for 20 minutes to allow flavours to absorb. Scatter coriander over the salad and serve.

Serves 2-3

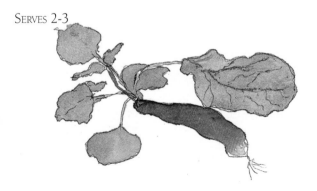

Potatoes and Pasta

Pasta Salad

Potato Salad

Mushroom Noodle Salad

Noodle, Mangetout and Red Pepper
with an Olive Dressing

Spiced Potato Salad

Pasta salad

You can use leftover pasta, however freshly cooked pasta is much better for absorbing the flavours and dressing.

225g (8oz) dried pasta – shells or twists are ideal
15mls (1 tbspn) olive oil
1 red pepper
1 yellow pepper
1 bunch of watercress, washed and chopped roughly
2 tomatoes, quartered
Half a bottle of Henderson's Tomato Dressing
Small pinch of salt
Freshly milled black pepper

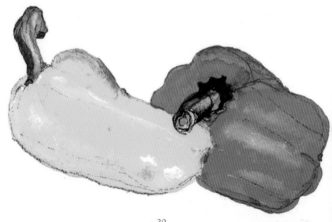

Method

Cook pasta in a pan of boiling lightly salted water, according to the instructions on the packet – usually about 12 minutes.

Meanwhile, chop the peppers, remove seeds and cut into generous chunks. Sauté quickly in olive oil over a high heat and allow to cool.

Drain pasta and combine all ingredients in a generously sized bowl. Ideally allow to stand for 30 minutes to allow flavours to absorb.

Serves 4

Potato salad

Like pasta, potatoes benefit from being warm when dressing is added.

Ingredients

225g (8oz) new potatoes, cooked and diced
1 red onion, peeled and finely chopped
15mls (1 tbspn) chopped parsley
100mls (4 fl oz) French dressing *(see dressings)*
Freshly milled black pepper

Method

Combine all ingredients in a bowl. Ideally allow to stand for 30 minutes to allow flavours to absorb.

Serves 2-3

Mushroom Noodle Salad

INGREDIENTS
100g (4oz) noodles
1 tspn vegetable bouillon stock
15mls (1 tbspn) olive oil
1 pepper, seeded and cut into strips
100g (4oz) mushrooms, quartered
1 courgette, chopped
1 clove of garlic, crushed
Small pinch of salt
Freshly milled black pepper
15mls (1 tbspn) chopped coriander

METHOD

Cook noodles according to the instructions on the packet adding the stock powder. Drain.

Meanwhile, heat olive oil in a pan and lightly sauté the vegetables for a few minutes.

Place noodles and vegetables, along with remaining ingredients into a large bowl. Toss and adjust seasoning to taste.

SERVES 2-3

Noodle, Mangetout and Red Pepper with an Olive Dressing

INGREDIENTS
1 sheet of noodles
15mls (1 tbspn) sunflower oil
1 red pepper, cut into 1cm slices
I clove garlic
50g (2oz) green olives, with stones removed
Small pinch of salt
Freshly milled black pepper
A generous bunch of basil, torn

METHOD
Cook noodles according to the instructions on the packet and drain.

Toss sliced peppers in the oil. Lift out and grill for a couple of minutes – ideally on a pre-heated chargrill pan. Blanch mangetout for a minute in boiling lightly salted water and drain.

Make a dressing with remaining oil by blitzing with the garlic and olives. Season to taste and combine all ingredients in a generously sized bowl. Toss to mix flavours thoroughly. Allow to stand for 30 minutes to allow flavours to absorb.

SERVES 2

Spiced Potato Salad

INGREDIENTS
225g (8oz) new potatoes, boiled
75g (3oz) green beans, halved and blanched
60mls (approx 4 tbspns) Spiced Dressing (*see Dressings*)
Small pinch of salt
Freshly milled black pepper

METHOD
Combine all ingredients in a bowl, cutting the potatoes into bite sized morsels. Ideally allow to stand for 30 minutes to allow flavours to absorb.

SERVES 2

Vegetables

Baked Butternut Squash, Rocket and Parmesan

Beetroot Salad

Carrot and Cheese Classic

Courgette and Walnut Salad

Henderson's Classic Coleslaw

Macedonia of Broccoli, Yellow Pepper, Tomato and Almonds

Marinated Mixed Mushrooms

Mediterranean Olive, Fennel and Mizuna with Cheese

Neapolitan Salad

Pepper, Orange and Olive Combo

Red Cabbage, Pear and Sesame Seed Salad

Roasted Root Vegetables in a Sweet Ginger Dressing

Thai Cucumber Salad

Trio of Baby Spinach, Red Chard and Nuts

Baked Butternut Squash, Rocket and Parmesan

INGREDIENTS
225g (8oz) butternut squash, peeled and diced
15mls (1 tbspn) olive oil
The juice of a lemon
Small pinch of salt
Freshly milled black pepper
100g (4oz) rocket, roughly torn
Shavings of Parmesan

METHOD
Pre-heat oven 190°C (375°F/Gas Mark 5).
Place squash on a roasting tray and drizzle with oil, some lemon juice and seasoning. Roast until tender but not mushy – approximately 15 minutes, depending on the size of chunks. Allow to cool.

Combine in a bowl with rocket and top with Parmesan shavings.

SERVES 2-3

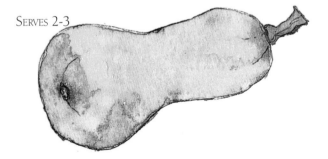

Beetroot Salad

INGREDIENTS
100g (4oz) beetroot, cooked and sliced
3 tomatoes, cut into wedges
1 bunch of watercress
15mls (1 tbspn) sesame seeds
Freshly milled pepper

METHOD
Wash and trim the watercress, removing lower stalk area.
Lightly toast the sesame seeds (optional).
    Combine all the ingredients in a generous bowl.

SERVES 2-3

Carrot and Cheese Classic

INGREDIENTS
2 medium carrots, scraped and grated
1 small red onion, sliced finely
6 tomatoes, cut into wedges
2 bunches of watercress
225g (8oz) cheddar cheese, grated

METHOD
Wash and trim the watercress, removing lower stalk area.
Combine all ingredients in a large bowl, mixing thoroughly
to blend flavours. This salad is best eaten promptly as
watercress has a tendency to wilt.

SERVES 4-6

Courgette and Walnut Salad

INGREDIENTS
225g (8oz) carrots, scraped and grated
2 medium courgettes, grated
75g (3oz) walnuts, roughly chopped
A few sprigs of fresh mint, chopped
The juice of a lemon

METHOD
In a large salad bowl, mix together all the ingredients and
serve as a fresh cleansing detox salad.

SERVES 4

Henderson's Classic Coleslaw

INGREDIENTS

Quarter of a cabbage, shredded
2 medium carrots, scraped and grated
30mls (2 tbspns) natural yoghurt
30mls (2 tbspns) mayonnaise
1 tbspn sesame seeds (optional)

METHOD

Combine all the ingredients in a bowl, coating the ingredients thoroughly with the dressing. Scatter with sesame seeds and serve immediately or chill.

SERVES 2-3

Macedonia of Broccoli, Yellow Pepper, Tomato, and Almonds

INGREDIENTS
100g (4oz) broccoli, cut into florets
1 yellow pepper, deseeded and cut into slivers
2 tomatoes, quartered
25g (1oz) almonds
Small pinch of salt
Freshly milled black pepper

METHOD
Blanch broccoli if wished in lightly salted boiling water for a moment. Drain and refresh with cold water (optional as it is delicious raw). Toast almonds to bring out flavour.

Combine all ingredients in a bowl and mix with your choice of dressing, or serve as it is.

SERVES 3

Marinated Mixed Mushrooms

INGREDIENTS

225g (8oz) Chestnut and/or button mushrooms, wiped, then
   quartered or sliced
30mls (2 tbspns) olive oil
The juice of a lemon
1 red onion, peeled and finely chopped
1 tbspn chopped chives
1 tbspn chopped parsley
Small pinch of salt
Freshly milled black pepper

METHOD

In a bowl, whisk oil with lemon juice and seasoning. Stir
and coat remaining ingredients and mushrooms and allow
flavours to absorb for at least 30 minutes. Stir once more
before serving.

Serves 2-3

Mediterranean Olive, Fennel, Mizuna, with Cheese

INGREDIENTS
1 fennel bulb, sliced finely
12 green olives
1 bag Mizuna
1 tbspn chopped parsley
100g (4oz) cheddar, diced
Half a cucumber (optional)
125mls (5 oz) French dressing

METHOD
Combine all ingredients in a bowl and mix thoroughly.
Allow flavours to absorb for 5 minutes before serving.

SERVES 2-3

Neapolitan Salad

225g (8oz) cauliflower, cut into florets
12 green olives
1 small red onion, peeled and sliced
10mls (1dtspn) capers
2 tomatoes, chopped
1 tbspn chopped parsley
1 tbspn chopped chives
30mls (2 tbspns) French dressing
Small pinch of salt

METHOD
Blanch cauliflower in a pan of
lightly salted boiling water.
Drain and refresh with cold
water to prevent further
cooking.

Combine all ingredients in
a generously sized bowl and
allow flavours to marinade for
10 minutes before serving.

SERVES 3-4

Pepper, Orange and Olive Combo

INGREDIENTS
2 oranges, peeled and diced
2 shallots, peeled and diced
1 red/yellow pepper, de-seeded and sliced
1 bunch watercress, washed, trimmed and chopped roughly
25g (1oz) stoned black olives, sliced
1 tbspn chopped Italian parsley
1 punnet cherry tomatoes, halved

METHOD
Combine all ingredients in a large mixing bowl and serve with your choice of dressing.

SERVES 2- 3

Red Cabbage, Pear and Sesame Seed Salad

INGREDIENTS
Half a medium sized red cabbage, cored and shredded
3 pears, cored and cut into bite sized chunks
1 tbspn sesame seeds
1 red pepper, sliced

METHOD:
Toast the sesame seeds to bring out the flavour.

In a bowl combine all the ingredients in a bowl and serve with a dressing of your choice (*see Dressings*).

SERVES 3-4

Roasted Root Vegetables in a Sweet Ginger Dressing

INGREDIENTS

1 sweet potato, peeled and cut into chunks

1 large baking potato, peeled and cut into chunks

2 medium carrots, scraped and diced

1 parsnip or similar sized piece of butternut squash, peeled
    and cut into chunks

30mls (2 tbspns) olive oil

50g (2oz) brown sugar

A walnut sized piece of root ginger, peeled and grated

Small pinch of salt

Freshly milled black pepper

125mls (4 fl oz) mayonnaise

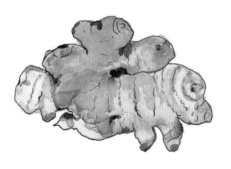

METHOD

Pre heat oven 190°C (375°F/Gas Mark 5). Scatter all the vegetables over a large roasting tray and drizzle with oil, sprinkle with ginger, sugar and seasoning.

Roast until tender but not mushy – approx 15 minutes, depending on the size of chunks, and allow to cool.

Place mayonnaise in a large bowl. Drain any cooking juices from the vegetables into the bowl and whisk.

Finally stir in vegetables and serve.

SERVES 3-4

Thai Cucumber Salad

INGREDIENTS

100g (4oz) cucumber
1 red onion, peeled and finely sliced
6 radishes, topped, tailed and sliced finely
1 tbspn sesame seeds
1 tbspn coriander, chopped
30mls (2 tbspns) Chilli Dressing (*see Dressings*)

METHOD

Using a potato peeler, cut cucumber into long fine ribbons. Place in a generously sized bowl with the dressing. Add onion, radish and seeds and combine. Leave to marinade for at least 10 minutes. Add coriander prior to serving

SERVES 2-3

Trio of Baby Spinach, Red Chard and Nuts

INGREDIENTS
1 pkt baby spinach leaves
A few mint leaves, chopped
25g (1oz) walnut pieces
45mls (3 tbspns) natural yoghurt
50g (2oz) green beans, cut in thirds
A few chard leaves
Juice of a lemon

METHOD
Toast the walnuts under a pre-heated grill to bring out
flavour. Blanch beans for a moment in lightly salted boiling
water, drain and refresh with cold water. Tear leaves into
bite sized morsels, combine with all ingredients in a bowl
and serve promptly.

SERVES 3

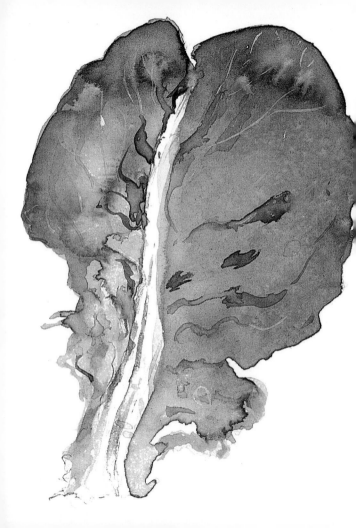

Leafy greens

Bistro Salad Platter

Herb Salad with Orange and Ginger

Saturday Salad

Bistro Salad Platter

INGREDIENTS
A selection of lettuce leaves
A few leaves of Mizuna and rocket
1 punnet mustard cress
Half a cucumber, sliced
2 tomatoes, cut in wedges

METHOD
Wash all leaves thoroughly and pat dry. Arrange in a bowl or platter. Snip halfway down mustard cress and scatter the tops over the leaves.

Arrange cucumber to evenly distribute through salad and finish off with tomatoes. Serve with a dressing of your choice (*see Dressings*).

SERVES 2-3

Herb Salad with Orange and Ginger

INGREDIENTS

Your choice of salad leaves (enough to fill a medium salad bowl) eg oak leaf, rocket, watercress, round lettuce.

The fruit segments and zest of an orange

A generous sprinkle of herbs eg chives, flat-leaf parsley, nasturtium etc.

100g (4oz) Coulommier or feta cheese

75mls (5 tbspns) olive oil

15mls (1 tbspn) balsamic vinegar

Small pinch of salt

Freshly milled black pepper

1 tspn blossom honey

1 tspn toasted sesame seeds

$1/4$ tspn peeled, finely grated root ginger

Prepare the leaves by washing and spinning/patting dry in advance. Place leaves (torn if large) and herbs in serving bowl, adding orange segments.

Dice cheese into bite sized morsels.

Combine all the other ingredients in a salad dressing jug, or a jam jar, apply stopper and shake well.

Dress the leaves just prior to serving. Any leftover dressing will keep in the fridge all week for future salads.

SERVES 2-4

54

Saturday Salad

Ingredients

10mls (1 dtspn) olive oil
Quarter of a fennel bulb, finely sliced
25g (1oz) mangetout
1 Cos lettuce
Several Radicchio leaves
A medium bunch of chives, chopped
Approx 10 rocket leaves
Quarter of cucumber, sliced
1 large slice Henderson's Nutty Malt Loaf, cut into cubes
45mls (3 tbspns) French Dressing

Method

In a pan lightly sauté the mangetout and fennel. Remove vegetables and add croûtons of bread. Coat lightly in remaining oil (add a little more if necessary) and cook croûtons until golden, taking care not to let them burn.

Tear assorted leaves into a large bowl. Add all remaining ingredients, mix together and serve. Cubes of cheddar cheese can be added to make this a main meal.

Serves 3

Dressings and Dips

Guacamole

INGREDIENTS
2 avocado, peeled, stoned and mashed
Quarter of a chilli, deseeded and diced
The juice of a lemon
1 clove garlic, peeled and crushed finely
Small pinch of salt
Freshly milled black pepper
Small bunch coriander, chopped
Drizzle of olive oil

METHOD
Combine all ingredients
in a bowl, mashing
to mix flavours but
keep some texture.
Delicious with
nachos.

Blue cheese dressing

INGREDIENTS
50mls olive oil
10mls (1dstsp) white wine vinegar
Small pinch of salt
Freshly milled black pepper
1 tspn wholegrain mustard
25g (1oz) mature blue cheese, crumbled eg Dunsyre Blue/
    Strathdon Blue
Dash of balsamic vinegar

METHOD
In a clean dressing bottle/jam jar, mix all ingredients
together. Replace lid and shake well. Keep refrigerated.

Chilli dressing

INGREDIENTS
60mls (4tbspns) olive oil
10mls (1dtspn) balsamic vinegar
1 tspn sugar
Half a chilli pepper, de-seeded and chopped finely

METHOD
Place all ingredients in a sterilized jar, screw on lid and
shake well.

French Dressing

50mls (3^1/$_2$ tbspns) olive oil
10mls (1dstsp) white wine vinegar
Small pinch of salt and freshly milled black pepper
1 tspn wholegrain mustard
1 tspn honey
Dash of balsamic vinegar

METHOD
Mix all ingredients together in a clean dressing bottle/jam
jar, replace lid and shake well.

Hummus

INGREDIENTS
225g (8oz) cooked chickpeas (canned work just as well)
1 clove garlic, peeled and crushed
Juice of a lemon
15mls (1 tbspn) olive oil
Small pinch of salt and freshly milled black pepper
Chopped parsley and coriander *(optional)*
Pinch of cayenne pepper *(optional)*
^{1}/$_2$ tspn of tahini *(optional)*

METHOD
Using a hand blender, or a fork, blend/mash all ingredients
except the herbs until as smooth as you like it. Scatter in
herbs and stir. Taste and adjust seasoning and lemon juice
according to your taste.

Spiced Dressing

INGREDIENTS
60mls (4 tbspns) olive oil
1 tbspn mixed herbs eg chopped basil, mint and marjoram
1 tspn Garam masala
A dash balsamic vinegar
Quarter of a chilli, deseeded and finely chopped

METHOD
In a clean dressing bottle/jam jar, mix all ingredients
together. Replace lid and shake well.

Fruits, Nuts and Sprouts

Banana, Cucumber and Cashew Nuts

Beansprout Salad

Carrot and Orange

Celery and Apple Salad

Fruit Coleslaw

Fruity Beansprout Salad.

Grapefruit, Mizuna Mix

Banana, Cucumber and Cashew Nuts

INGREDIENTS
Half a cucumber, cut into chunks
2 bananas, peeled and sliced in chunks
50g (2oz) cashew nuts
100mls (6¹/₂ tbspns) soured cream

METHOD
Toast cashews on a tray under a medium
high grill to bring out flavour then allow to cool.
Combine all ingredients in a bowl and serve.

SERVES 2-3

Beansprout Salad

INGREDIENTS

75g (3oz) beansprouts
75g (3oz) beanshoots
1pkt (250g) tofu, diced
25g (1oz) coriander, chopped
1 carrot, grated
1 tbspn poppy seeds
1 yellow pepper, de-seeded and sliced
A walnut sized piece of fresh ginger, peeled and grated
Drizzle of olive oil

METHOD

To prepare sprouting seeds and
beans, tease them out and rinse
under a cold tap. Shake out
the excess water using a sieve.
In a large bowl, mix all the
ingredients and toss to
combine the flavours
completely. Keep chilled
until ready to serve as sprouts
will lose their crisp refreshing
taste if left out too long in
a hot kitchen.

SERVES 4-6

Carrot and Orange

INGREDIENTS
3 medium sized (approx 225g/8oz) carrots, grated
2 oranges, peeled and diced
2 tomatoes, chopped
1 bunch watercress
25g (1oz) raisins
1 tbspn sunflower seeds

METHOD
Wash and trim the watercress, removing lower stalk area.
Combine all ingredients in a bowl, mixing well.

SERVES 3-4

Fruit Coleslaw

INGREDIENTS
Half a cabbage, shredded
2 apples, cored and diced
75g (3oz) raisins
45mls (3 tbspn) natural yoghurt
45mls (3 tbspn) mayonnaise

METHOD
Combine all the ingredients in a bowl, coating the
ingredients thoroughly with the dressing. Serve
immediately or chill.

SERVES 2-3

Celery and Apple Salad

100g (4oz) celery, sliced
1 red apple, cored and cut into chunks
50g (2oz) hazelnuts
15mls (1 tbspn) mayonnaise
15mls (1 tbspn) natural yoghurt

METHOD
Combine all ingredients in a large bowl and serve
immediately or chill.

SERVES 2

Fruity Beansprout Salad.

INGREDIENTS
175g (6oz) beansprouts
1 dtspn sesame seeds
1 orange, peeled and sliced
1 carrot, scraped and grated
3 spring onions, top, tailed and sliced
Juice of half a lemon

METHOD:
To prepare sprouts, tease them out
and rinse under a cold tap. Shake out
the excess water using a sieve. Combine
all ingredients in a large serving bowl
and serve.

SERVES 2

Grapefruit and Mizuna Mix

INGREDIENTS
2 pink grapefruits, peeled and segmented
100g (4oz) Mizuna/Mustard Leaf
25g (1oz) sultanas
25g (1oz) sunflower seeds
25g (1oz) pumpkin seeds

METHOD
Combine all ingredients in a large mixing bowl, tearing larger leaves into manageable bites.

SERVES 2

Refreshing Juices

Definitely detox! Deliciously healthy. A hand-held blitzer is best for these juices. Remember to remove any seeds, pips, stones or cores.

CARROT, APPLE AND GINGER JUICE

MANGO AND BANANA QUENCHER

MELON AND PINEAPPLE JUICE

MELON, PEAR AND APPLE JUICE

PAPAYA AND BANANA JUICE

PLUM AND PEAR NECTAR

RASPBERRY AND BANANA SMOOTHIE

STRAWBERRY AND BANANA JUICE

Carrot, Apple and Ginger Juice

INGREDIENTS
2 medium carrots, peeled and washed
2 apples, cored
560mls (1 pint) orange juice
$^1/_2$ tspn peeled and finely grated ginger

METHOD
Chop apples and carrots into chunks to blend. Place these in a beaker, add orange juice and blend until as smooth as possible. Mix in grated ginger.

SERVES 4-6

Mango and Banana Quencher

INGREDIENTS
1 mango, peeled and cut away from stone
2 bananas, peeled and broken up
560mls (1 pint) orange juice

METHOD
Place all the ingredients in the blender beaker and blitz
until smooth.

SERVES 4

Melon and Pineapple Juice

INGREDIENTS
1 melon, peeled, pipped and roughly cut into chunks
1 pineapple, peeled, cored and cut into chunks
1 litre (1^3/$_4$ pints) orange juice
a few mint leaves

METHOD
Place all the ingredients in the blender beaker and blitz until smooth. You may need to do this in two batches depending on the size of the beaker.

SERVES 4-6

Melon, Pear and Apple Juice

INGREDIENTS
Half a melon, peeled and pipped
2 pears, quartered and cored.
1 apple, cored and peeled if wished
300mls (^{1}/$_2$ pint) apple juice

METHOD
Place all the ingredients in the blender beaker and blitz until smooth.

SERVES 4

Strawberry and Banana Juice

INGREDIENTS
450g (1lb) strawberries, hulled
2 bananas, peeled and broken up
1 litre (1³/₄ pints) orange juice

METHOD
Place all the ingredients in the blender beaker and blitz until smooth. You may need to do this in two batches depending on the size of the beaker.

SERVES 4-6

Papaya and Banana Juice

INGREDIENTS
1 papaya, peeled and pipped
2 bananas, peeled and broken up
560mls (1 pint) orange juice

METHOD
Place all the ingredients in the blender beaker and blitz
until smooth.

SERVES 4

Plum and Pear Nectar

INGREDIENTS
2 plums, stoned
1 pear, cored
300mls ($^1/_2$ pint) orange juice

METHOD
Place all the ingredients in the blender beaker and blitz
until smooth. Depending on the season, plums may have
a coarser skin. In this case you may wish to pass juice
through a sieve to remove flecks of skin prior to serving.

SERVES 3-4

Raspberry and Banana Smoothie

INGREDIENTS
100g (4oz) raspberries
1 banana, peeled and broken up
300mls ($^1/_2$ pint) orange juice *or* natural unsweetened
yoghurt

METHOD
Place all the ingredients in the blender beaker
and blitz until smooth.

SERVES 3-4

Conversion Tables

The following tables are the approximate conversions for metric and imperial measures used throughout this book. All are approximate conversions, which have either been rounded up or down. It is important not to mix metric and imperial measures, stick to one system or the other. Henderson's chefs use standard cups (8 fl oz) as an easy and convenient measure.

WEIGHTS		VOLUME	
$1/2$oz	15g	1 fl oz	25ml
1oz	25g	2 fl oz	50ml
2oz	50g	3 fl oz	75ml
3oz	75g	5 fl oz ($1/4$ pint)	150ml
4oz	110g	10 fl oz ($1/2$ pint)	275ml
5oz	150g	15 fl oz ($3/4$ pint)	400ml
6oz	175g	1 pint	570ml
7oz	200g	$1^1/4$ pints	700ml
8oz	225g	$1^1/2$ pints	900ml
9oz	250g	$1^3/4$ pints	1 litres
10oz	275g	2 pints	1.1 litres
11oz	310g	$2^1/4$ pints	1.3 litres
12oz	350g	$2^1/2$ pints	1.4 litres
13oz	375g	3 pints	1.75 litres
14oz	400g	$3^1/4$ pints	1.8 litres
15oz	425g	$3^1/2$ pints	2 litres
1lb	450g	$3^3/4$ pints	2.1 litres
$1^1/4$lb	550g	4 pints	2.3 litres
$1^1/2$lb	700g	5 pints	2.8 litres
2lb	900g	6 pints	3.4 litres
3lb	1.4kg	7 pints	4 litres
4lb	1.8kg	8 pints	4.5 litres
5lb	2.3kg		

MEASUREMENTS

$^1/_4$in	$^1/_2$cm
$^1/_2$in	1cm
1in	$2^1/_2$cm
2in	5cm
3in	$7^1/_2$cm
4in	10cm
6in	15cm
7in	18cm
8in	$20^1/_2$cm
9in	23cm

OVEN TEMPERATURES

275°F	140°C	Gas Mark 1
300°F	150°C	Gas Mark 2
325°F	170°C	Gas Mark 3
350°F	180°C	Gas Mark 4
375°F	190°C	Gas Mark 5
400°F	200°C	Gas Mark 6
425°F	220°C	Gas Mark 7
450°F	230°C	Gas Mark 8
475°F	240°C	Gas Mark 9